P is for Playdate

P is for Playdate
Published by Kinkajou

Reproduced courtesy of Yellow House Art Licensing
www.yellowhouseartlicensing.com

A catalogue record for this book is available from the British Library

Kinkajou is an imprint of Frances Lincoln Limited
74–77 White Lion Street
London N1 9PF
www.kinkajou.com

ISBN: 978-0-7112-3715-5

Printed in China

FSC
www.fsc.org
MIX
Paper from
responsible sources
FSC® C104723

P is for Playdate

A Modern Parent's Guide
to Surviving Your Child's Social Life

By Joel Rickett & Spencer Wilson

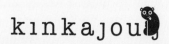

Allergies

Most children know if there is something they are not allowed to eat… but if they go rogue, you need to be prepared. Ask in advance to avoid the unwitting supply of banned substances.

Arguments

Three's a crowd. When planning a playdate, remember that two, four or even five kids are easier to manage than three.

If they're constantly sniping at each other, the solution might be simple: snacks, TV or a heady mixture of both.

B

Baking

Make up a batch of cookie dough in advance for your kids to roll out, cut into shapes and bake. Or you can start from scratch but be prepared for the consequences (see C for Crime Scene). Cookie dough will keep in the fridge for a couple of days. It can also be frozen, either in ready-to-bake blobs, or in batches to be defrosted and rolled out.

simple cookie dough:

225g (8oz) soft butter
140g (5oz) golden caster sugar
280g (10oz) plain flour
1 egg yolk & a pinch of salt

Cream together the butter and sugar until light and fluffy. Beat in the egg and then add the flour and salt. To flavour your cookies add either 1-2 tsps. vanilla essence, orange/lemon zest or chocolate chips. You can also add peanut butter or swap out some of the flour for ground almonds.

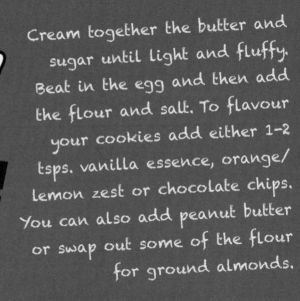

Bug Hunt

When the weather's on your side, allowing your children to grub around in the garden or local park can offer hours of fun.

Make a temporary bug home using a transparent plastic beaker, a piece of paper or plastic pierced with breathing holes for a roof and a rubber band to keep it in place. Have a magnifying glass handy to examine the bugs close up, and some pencils and paper to draw and log any interesting discoveries to be identified later.

N.B. You will be lobbied to bring the bugs indoors. Resist.

C

Crime Scene

What a room may resemble after it has been inhabited for more than a minute by a bunch of unsupervised children. As in most crime scenes, detection of who is responsible for what is not straightforward; all suspects will deny involvement...

Den

The simple kind of fun we used to have pre-DVDs.

Disco

Dim the lights and use torches to create a late night feel. Ramp up the stereo and retreat.

Dress Up

A large old suitcase filled with clothes and props provides hours of fun. Superhero and princess costumes are always a winner and the resulting role-play can be entertaining (but not if there are weapons).

DVD

Long run times rule, and the old Disney classics did not stint on those. Have a 'classic' to hand at all times.

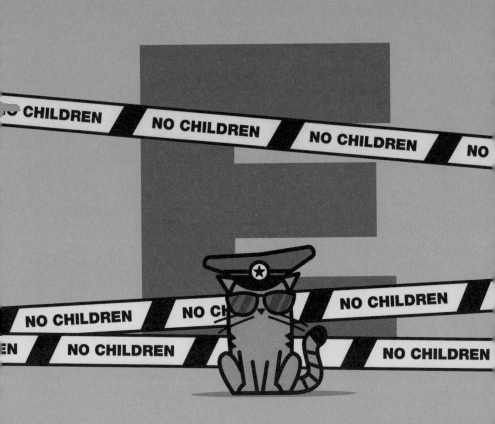

Exclusion Zone

If you are lucky enough to have the space for lots of guests, it's useful to preserve a quiet room of the house. This is where you and your fellow parents huddle, with coffees, teas, or a glass of something with more kick.

Facepaint

Older kids just love to express their creative sides by daubing facepaint on any younger (willing) victims. Make sure you buy good stuff so they don't reach for the poster paints.

Game Plan

Tool yourself up. You never know what will be needed. If adult intervention becomes necessary, Musical Statues, Simon Says or Sleeping Lions can all be organised at short notice.

Try this: Animal Antics

Write the names of animals on pieces of paper and ask each child to choose one without looking. Stick the names of the animals on the children's foreheads so that everybody else can see it except them. Each child then takes it in turn to ask one of the others to act out the animal that they are, so that they can guess.

PIG

Handprints

Not for the fainthearted. This activity should be carried out with military precision or you will suffer the consequences for days/weeks/years (see C for Crime Scene).

House Envy

A natural consequence of your child's busy social life is getting a glimpse inside other family homes. Some will seem impossibly well-appointed and clean. But remember it's largely an illusion; they'll have been up all night to create an impression of affluent calm. Your own kind of domestic chaos is far more healthy. Definitely.

I

Pretty much the only acceptable
dessert at a playdate.
N.B. Toppings are now mandatory:
biscuits
melted chocolate
bananas
raspberrys
granola
marshmallows
M&Ms

iPaddy

In any gathering of kids, possession of the tablet-device is all-important. It will confer instant celebrity status and power. They must learn to wield the power benignly.

Tablet tips:
1) Try to hide them before the event.
2) If 1) fails, try to keep en eye on what they're watching or playing. In a couple of clicks, a harmless episode of Sesame Street can become a Miley Cyrus video.

Juice

**Kids love it, but beware:
things can get sticky.
Always keep a bulk supply
of wet wipes nearby (see W).**

K

Ketchup

One of their five a day. Use liberally
and marvel at how rejected lunch items
suddenly become acceptable.

Lego

The undisputed champion of play. But beware the Lego minefield.

A good reason to wear slippers.

M

Meltdown

Remember: be tough on meltdowns and tough on the causes of meltdowns. See V for Variety and S for Snacks for more guidance.

N
Natural Play

Sometimes known as 'wild time',

this is what we all did for most of our own childhoods. Whether it's a park, a forest or an urban garden, the principle is the same: make your own fun in glorious communion with nature.

When this goes well it's blissful: kids happily digging for beetles, climbing trees, and picking berries.

When it goes wrong, torrential rain drenches everyone, sticks are wielded as weapons, and a Lord of the Flies-style anarchy quickly reigns.

www.projectwildthing.com/wildtime
www.ted.com/talks/gever_tulley_on_5_dangerous_things_for_kids

O Offload

Around the age of four or five, it becomes acceptable to start leaving your children at playdates and parties.

The first time this happens it is a miracle, and you wander around in a daze. You quickly learn to ruthlessly exploit the opportunity.

So yes, playdates can provide free childcare... but remember that you need to reciprocate. Soon the tide will turn and a bunch of kids will be dumped on you. Which is where this book comes in useful...

Outbreak

If one child has a cough or cold, a playdate or party creates the perfect conditions to ensure its fast and furious transferral. Most of the time this is unavoidable, but for tummy bugs the only possible policy is zero tolerance.

P

Pesto

What did parents do without Pesto?

Pizza

See above.

Potion

Sometimes referred to as 'mixture', these are the murky concoctions that kids love to stir up.

Peanut butter, soap, toothpaste, vinegar, cologne... everything goes into the mix.

These are often in progress when all goes suspiciously quiet (see next entry).

Quiet

**As in suspiciously so.
The moment that you realise you
haven't heard anything from upstairs
for what seems like hours.**

That means they're up to
something.

Who's brave enough to
go and take a look?

Rules

Treat each other with respect

No shouting

No chewing gum

No heavy weaponry

Show

Encourage their dramatic sides. The results are best enjoyed when coinciding with W (Wine Time).

Supplies

Kids:
Juice (several varieties)
Carrot sticks
Cucumber
Pitta bread
Cookies
Ice cream
Pasta
Pesto
Hummus

Grown-ups:
Paracetamol
Ear-plugs
Bottle of wine (see W for Wine Time)

(No) Scrapping

It starts off with a playful tumble. Swiftly progressing to a scuffle. If left unchecked, it'll soon become all-out cage fighting.

Time Out

The new classic of parental discipline. But wield it carefully, especially on a playdate. See M for Meltdown and U for Unreasonable.

Unreasonable

Dictators and mafia bosses have been known to be less demanding and fairer than some of the behaviour you may see at a playdate…

Variety

As all professional kids party entertainers know, managing the crowd is all-important.

Any gathering will need variation in tempo. Alternate between physical activities, quieter games, and screen time – and keep a good flow of snacks.

The moment you get complacent is the moment things go wrong (see M for Meltdown).

Vomit

Always a dramatic conclusion to any social gathering. See A for Allergy, X for eXcess and O for Outbreak.

Wet Wipes

Never, ever hold a playdate without them. Ever.

Wine Time

Many family houses have an unofficial Wine Time – the moment when the kids finally settle in bed and a bottle can be uncorked to mark the end of another epic day.

On a playdate, *Wine Time* can be virtually any time. Parents huddle in the kitchen clutching their drinks, as anarchy reigns elsewhere. Monday, 11am? Sure, I'll have a small glass.

eXcess

You put out a bowl of chips and one child necks the **WHOLE** lot. Smaller quantities result in smaller acts of greed – limit the amount available.

Yummy Mummy

There's always one.
While most parents arrive at the
school gate looking unkempt and
barely dressed, some simply glide
in. Whatever the weather, they
are sculpted and perfumed.

They must have nannies.
At least two per child.

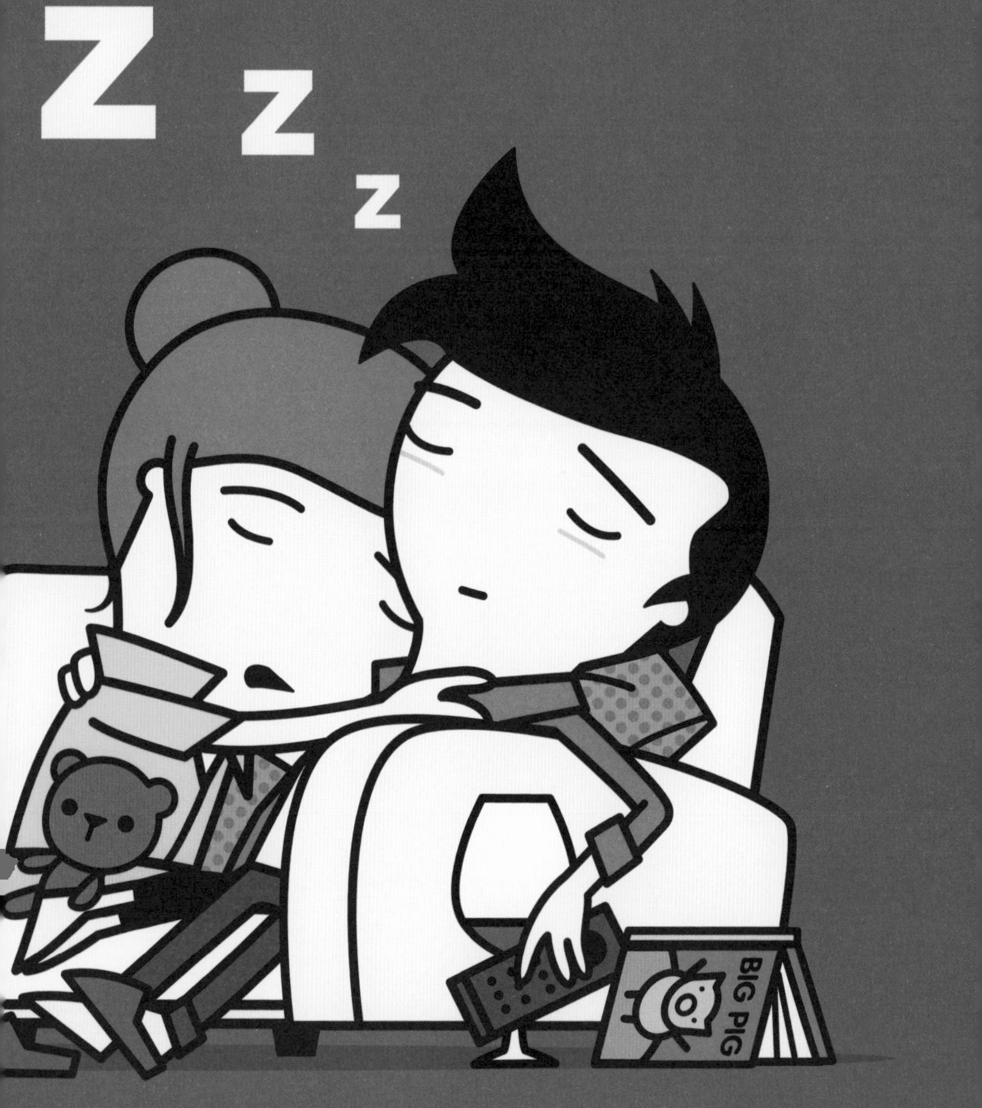
Z
Z
Z
BIG PIG

Notes

Buy Sweets

P

Playdate

P is for Playdate

To: _____

From: _____

Day: _____

Time: _____

Place: _____

_____

_____

_____

_____

RSVP: _____

Email: _____

P

Playdate

P is for Playdate

To: _____

From: _____

Day: _____

Time: _____

Place: _____

_____

_____

_____

_____

RSVP: _____

Email: _____

P

Playdate

P is for Playdate

To: _____

From: _____

Day: _____

Time: _____

Place: _____

_____

_____

_____

_____

RSVP: _____

Email: _____

P

Playdate

P is for Playdate

To: _____

From: _____

Day: _____

Time: _____

Place: _____

_____

_____

_____

_____

RSVP: _____

Email: _____

P

Playdate

P is for Playdate

To: _____

From: _____

Day: _____

Time: _____

Place: _____

_____

_____

_____

_____

RSVP: _____

Email: _____

P

Playdate

P is for Playdate

To: _____

From: _____

Day: _____

Time: _____

Place: _____

_____

_____

_____

_____

RSVP: _____

Email: _____

P

Playdate

P is for Playdate

To: _____

From: _____

Day: _____

Time: _____

Place: _____

_____

_____

_____

_____

RSVP: _____

Email: _____

Playdate

P is for Playdate

To: _____

From: _____

Day: _____

Time: _____

Place: _____

_____

_____

_____

RSVP: _____

Email: _____

P

Playdate

P is for Playdate

To: _____

From: _____

Day: _____

Time: _____

Place: _____

_____

_____

_____

_____

RSVP: _____

Email: _____

P

Playdate

P is for Playdate

To: _____

From: _____

Day: _____

Time: _____

Place: _____

_____

_____

_____

_____

RSVP: _____

Email: _____

P

Playdate

P is for Playdate

To: _____

From: _____

Day: _____

Time: _____

Place: _____

_____

_____

_____

_____

RSVP: _____

Email: _____

P
Playdate

P

P is for Playdate

To: _____

From: _____

Day: _____

Time: _____

Place: _____

_____

_____

_____

_____

RSVP: _____

Email: _____

Playdate

P is for Playdate

To: _____

From: _____

Day: _____

Time: _____

Place: _____

_____

_____

_____

_____

RSVP: _____

Email: _____

P

Playdate

P is for Playdate

To: _____

From: _____

Day: _____

Time: _____

Place: _____

_____

_____

_____

RSVP: _____

Email: _____

P

Playdate

P is for Playdate

To: _____

From: _____

Day: _____

Time: _____

Place: _____

_____

_____

_____

_____

RSVP: _____

Email: _____

P

Playdate

P is for Playdate

To: _____

From: _____

Day: _____

Time: _____

Place: _____

_____

_____

_____

_____

RSVP: _____

Email: _____

Playdate

P is for Playdate

To: _____

From: _____

Day: _____

Time: _____

Place: _____

_____

_____

_____

_____

RSVP: _____

Email: _____

Playdate

P is for Playdate

To: _____

From: _____

Day: _____

Time: _____

Place: _____

_____

_____

_____

_____

RSVP: _____

Email: _____

Playdate

P is for Playdate

To: _____

From: _____

Day: _____

Time: _____

Place: _____

_____

_____

_____

_____

RSVP: _____

Email: _____

P

Playdate

P is for Playdate

To: _____

From: _____

Day: _____

Time: _____

Place: _____

_____

_____

_____

_____

RSVP: _____

Email: _____

P

Playdate

P is for Playdate

To: _____

From: _____

Day: _____

Time: _____

Place: _____

_____

_____

_____

_____

RSVP: _____

Email: _____

T

Thank you

...is for Thank you

Thank you

...is for Thank you

T

Thank you

...is for Thank you

T

Thank you

...is for Thank you

T

Thank you

...is for Thank you

Thank you

...is for Thank you

T

Thank you

...is for Thank you

_____

_____

_____

_____

_____

_____

_____

_____

_____

_____

_____

T

Thank you

...is for Thank you

T

Thank you

...is for Thank you

Thank you

...is for Thank you

T

Thank you

...is for Thank you

T

Thank you

...is for Thank you

T

Thank you

...is for Thank you

Thank you

...is for Thank you

T

Thank you

...is for Thank you

T

Thank you

...is for Thank you

Thank you

...is for Thank you

_____

_____

_____

_____

_____

_____

_____

_____

_____

_____

_____

_____

Thank you

...is for Thank you

T

Thank you

...is for Thank you